LET'S LEARN ABOUT...
THE OCEAN

PROJECT BOOK

PERSONAL, SOCIAL, AND EMOTIONAL DEVELOPMENT

K1

P Pearson

Pearson Education Limited
KAO Two, KAO Park, Harlow, Essex, CM17 9NA, England
and Associated Companies around the world

First published 2020
Third impression 2021

ISBN: 978-12-9233-406-6

Set in Mundo Sans
Printed in Slovakia by Neografia.

Acknowledgements
The publishers and author(s) would like to thank the following people and institutions for their feedback and comments during the development of the material: Marcos Mendonça, Leandra Dias, Viviane Kirmeliene, Gisele Aga, Rhiannon Ball, Simara H. Dal'Alba, Mônica Bicalho and GB Editorial. The publishers would also like to thank all the teachers who contributed to the development of *Let's learn about...*: Adriano de Paula Souza, Aline Ramos Teixeira Santo, Aline Vitor Rodrigues Pina Pereira, Ana Paula Gomez Montero, Anna Flávia Feitosa Passos, Camila Jarola, Celiane Junker Silva, Edegar França Junior, Fabiana Reis Yoshio, Fernanda de Souza Thomaz, Luana da Silva, Michael Iacovino Luidvinavicius, Munique Dias de Melo, Priscila Rossatti Duval Ferreira Neves, Sandra Ferito, and schools that took part in Construindo Juntos.

Author Acknowledgements
Angela Llanas, Libby Williams, Karina Sanghikian, Lisiane Ott Schulz, Luciana Pinheiro

Image Credit(s):
Pearson Education Ltd: Olivia González 67; **Shutterstock.com:** 11, A_Lesik 47, Aksinia Abiagam 19, 19, Aleksei Martynov 17, All-stock-photos 53, Andrey_Kuzmin 53, antoniodiaz 9, Asier Romero 19, Bachkova Natalia 47, Boris Medvedev 61, Chanawee Champakerdthapya 65, CKA 65, cristi180884 53, Darren Baker 11, DGLimages 37, Dmytro Surkov 49, Dragan Grkic 37, Drpixel 25, Dudarev Mikhail 47, effective stock photos 47, Emese 11, Eric Isselee 47, Erika Cross 5, ESB Professional 65, fizkes 5, Flashon Studio 61, FrameStockFootages 25, Gaidamashchuk 17, Galina Gutarin 9, HorenkO 9, India Picture 25, Iryna Afonina 17, 17, Ivonne Wierink 61, Jan Mlkvy 65, Kichigin 49, Lena Bukovsky 17, LightField Studios 25, Maks Narodenko 53, Malvales 17, Michael Kraus 61, Monkey Business Images 25, NeydtStock 65, Nicescene 61, NikolayTsyu 47, Oksana Kuzmina 37, Ole_CNX 37, 37, Pixel-Shot 43, Pressmaster 5, Ravennka 47, Rawpixel.com 43, Regreto 33, Robert Kneschke 65, Ronnachai Palas 43, Sand T Laovanichvit 65, ScofieldZa 65, SLP_London 61, Sofi photo 5, stockcreations 53, Suthiporn Hanchana 61, Tanya_mtv 61, Tatyana Dzemileva 33, Toey Toey 9, Tursk Aleksandra 25, Valentina Razumova 53, Vangert 47, Vladimir Nenezic 65, World of Vector 17, Yellow Cat 33, Yuliya Evstratenko 9, ZouZou 11

Illustration Acknowledgements
Illustrated by MRS Editorial and Filipe Laurentino

Cover illustration © Filipe Laurentino

CONTENTS

CIRCLE THE CORRECT WORD.

HELLO.

GOODBYE.

HELLO.

GOODBYE.

PLEASE.

THANKS.

PLEASE.

THANKS.

SPIN A PENCIL IN THE MIDDLE OF THE CIRCLE. MIME THE EMOTIONS. 🏐

THINK!
WHAT GAMES DO YOU LIKE TO PLAY?

TALK ABOUT THE PICTURES. THEN MATCH.

THINK!
WHAT DO YOU DO WHEN YOU ARE HAPPY/SAD?

TALK ABOUT THE PICTURES. CIRCLE THE THINGS THAT YOU SHARE WITH YOUR FRIENDS.

THINK!
HOW DO YOU FEEL WHEN YOU SHARE YOUR THINGS?

LISTEN AND STICK.

LISTEN TO YOUR TEACHER. PLAY THE GAME AND STICK.

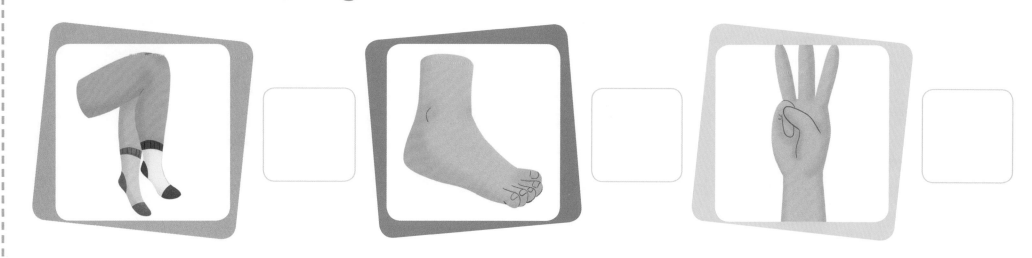

LISTEN TO YOUR TEACHER. PLAY THE GAME.

MATCH THE BOY'S FRONT WITH HIS BACK.

DRAW YOUR FACE. LISTEN.

ARE YOU A GOOD FAMILY MEMBER? COLOR THE RIGHT FACE.

ARE YOU A GOOD FRIEND? COLOR THE RIGHT FACE.

POINT TO THE FAMILY MEMBERS.

DRAW YOUR FAMILY MEMBERS.

DRAW A STAR NEXT TO THE FAMILY THAT IS SIMILAR TO YOURS. SAY.

THINK!
WHO DO YOU LIVE WITH?

ARE YOU A GOOD FAMILY MEMBER? STICK THE CORRECT FACE.

ARE YOU A GOOD FRIEND? STICK THE CORRECT FACE.

LOOK. ORDER THE STORY.

CIRCLE THE TOYS YOU LIKE TO PLAY WITH.

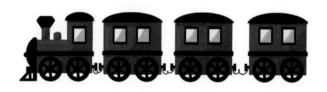

COUNT THE TOYS YOU LIKE TO PLAY WITH.
CIRCLE THE NUMBER.

1 2 3 4 5 6

WHAT ARE THE CHILDREN DOING?

DRAW ANOTHER PLAY-TOGETHER TOY.

THINK!
HOW DO YOU FEEL WHEN SOMEONE SHARES WITH YOU?

CIRCLE THE PICTURE WHERE THE GIRL IS KIND.

THINK!
HOW KIND ARE YOU TO OTHERS?

CHECK THE CHORES YOU DO.
CROSS OUT THE CHORES YOU DON'T DO.

COMPARE WITH A FRIEND.

WHO HELPS AT HOME? CHECK.

DO YOU MAKE YOUR OWN BED? LISTEN AND ORDER THE PICTURES.

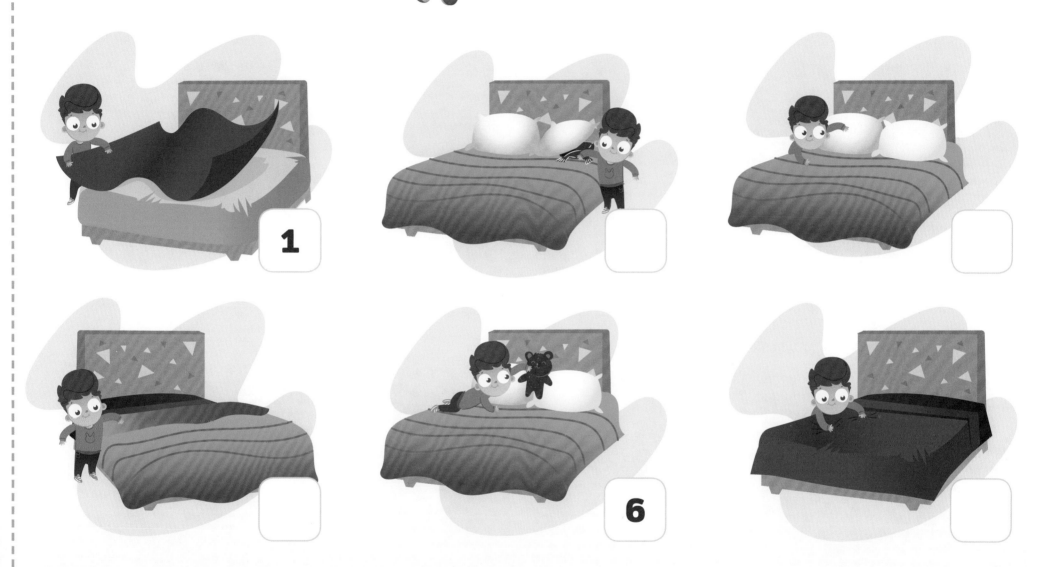

WHAT TOYS DO YOU SLEEP WITH?

TALK ABOUT THE PICTURES. ACT OUT THE SITUATIONS. 👄

DRAW WHAT YOU DO TO HELP AT HOME. ✏️

THINK!
WHAT CHORES ARE FUN TO DO?

LISTEN AND NUMBER THE PICTURES.

MATCH EACH ANIMAL WITH THEIR HABITAT.

IS EVERYONE KIND TO ANIMALS?
WHAT DO PETS NEED?

WHAT ANIMALS NEED HELP? CIRCLE.

LOOK AT THE PICTURE. WHO IS A VET?
WHAT DOES A VET DO?

CIRCLE WHAT A DOCTOR DOES.

THINK!
WHEN DO YOU SEE A DOCTOR?

WHAT DOES MAX LIKE?
WHAT DOESN'T MAX LIKE? MATCH.

CHECK THE THINGS YOU LIKE.
CROSS OUT THE THINGS YOU DON'T LIKE.

COLOR THE HEALTHY FOOD.

LOOK AT THE PICTURE AND LISTEN.

WHAT DOES DIANA NEED TO DO? STICK.

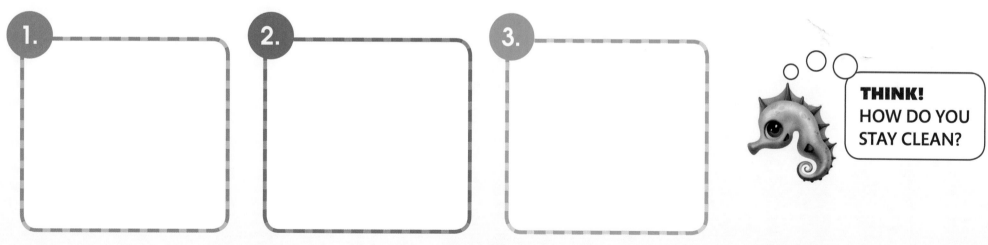

1.

2.

3.

THINK!
HOW DO YOU STAY CLEAN?

LISTEN. CIRCLE THE FOOD SOME CHILDREN DON'T LIKE. 🎧 07 ✏️

DRAW FOOD YOU LIKE FOR YOUR PARTY. ✏️

THINK!
DO YOU SHARE FOOD WITH YOUR FRIENDS? WHY?

LISTEN. MATCH THE TOYS WITH THE CHILDREN. 🎧 ⬧

DRAW YOURSELF WITH YOUR FAVORITE TOY. ✏️

LISTEN. FIND MATT, ALLIE, SAM, AND OLIVE.

DRAW YOURSELF IN THE SANDBOX.

LISTEN AND MOVE YOUR COUNTER.
SAY THE NUMBER AND THE WORD.

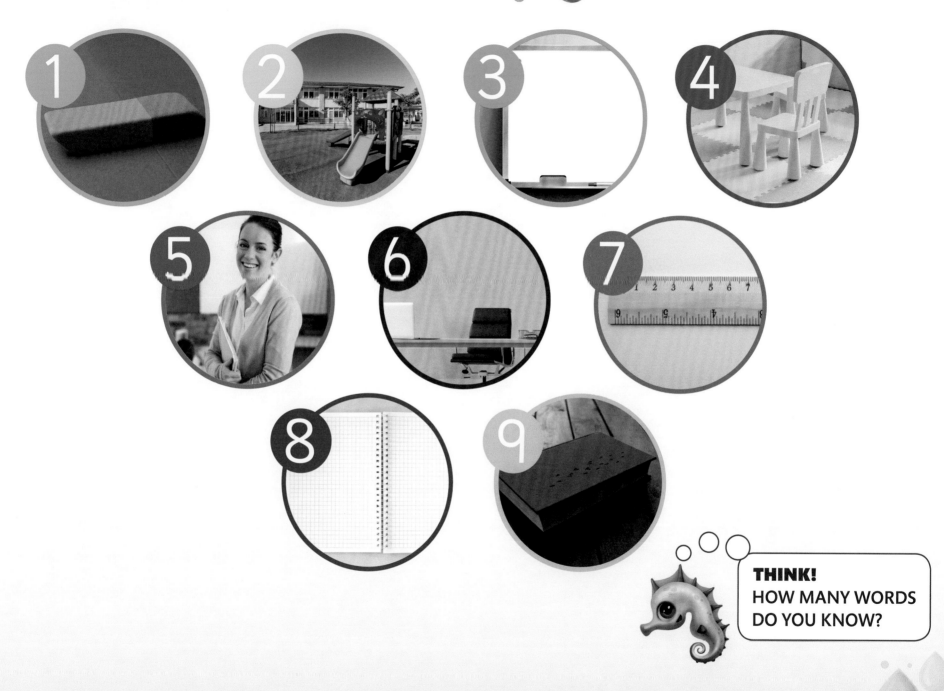

THINK!
HOW MANY WORDS
DO YOU KNOW?

ARE THE CHILDREN BEING NICE TO EACH OTHER? COLOR.

THINK! HOW CAN YOU BE NICE TO SOMEONE TODAY?

DRAWING

DRAW.

DRAW.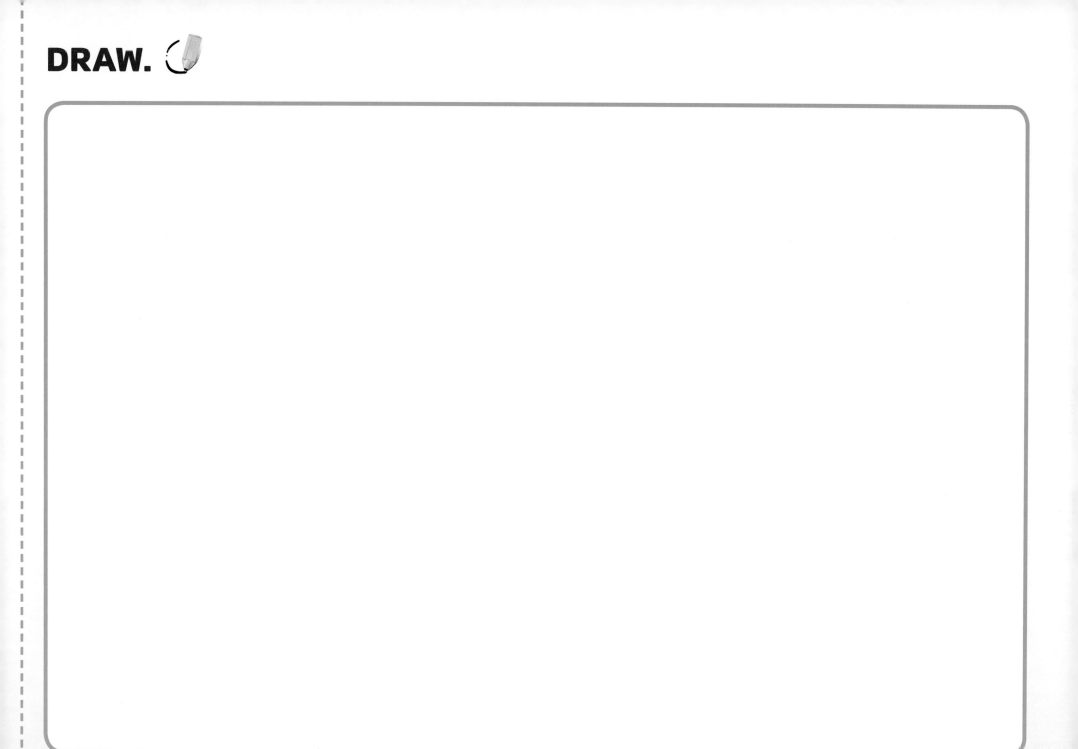

DRAW.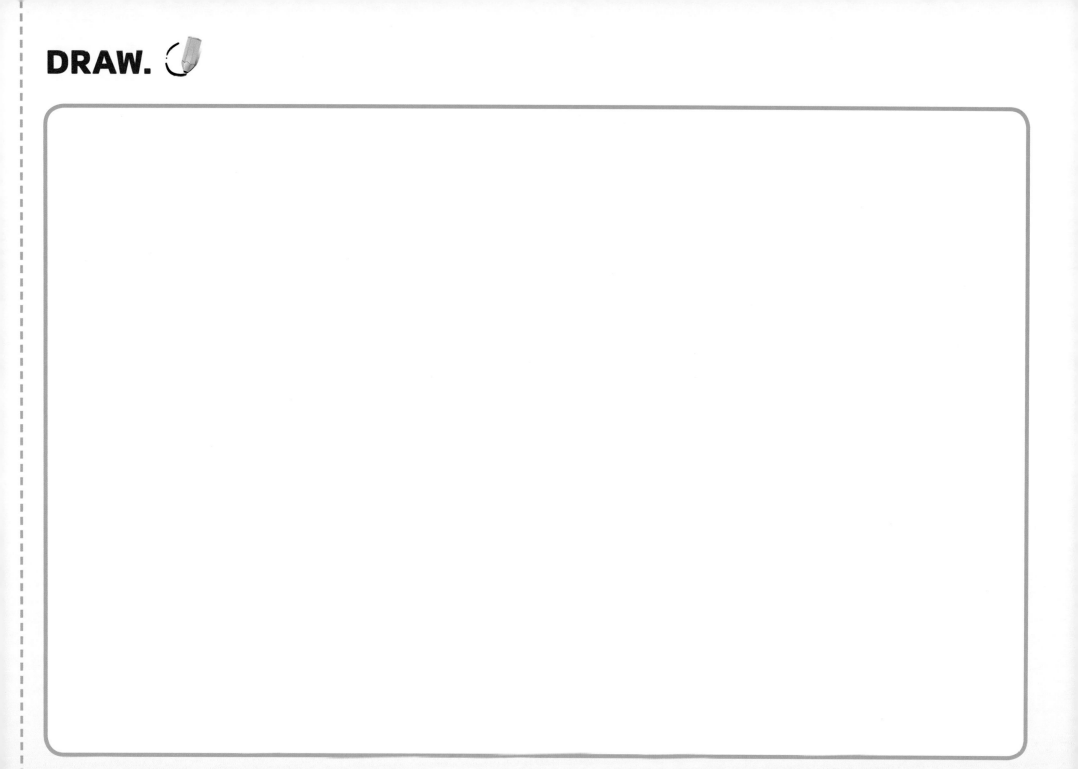

DRAW.

DRAW.

STICKERS

STICKERS

UNIT 2

1

2

3

UNIT 3

UNIT 7

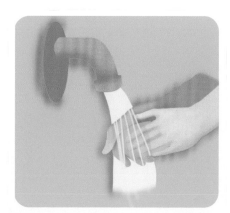